# Contents

What did the Tudors do for me? ......................4

What was daily life like in Tudor times? ...........8

How were the Tudors educated? ....................12

What did the Tudors do for entertainment? ...14

How did society change under
    the Tudors? ...............................................20

Where did the Tudors explore
    and trade?..................................................24

Key dates...................................................28

Glossary.....................................................30

Find out more.............................................31

Index.........................................................32

Look for the Then and Now boxes. They highlight parts of Tudor culture that are present in our modern world.

Any words appearing in the text in bold, **like this**, are explained in the glossary.

# What did the Tudors do for me?

Between 1485 and 1603, a family called the Tudors ruled England. These kings and queens, or **monarchs**, reigned at a time of great change. During the Tudor period, many people became wealthier and towns grew rapidly. William Shakespeare wrote his famous plays, and adventurers explored and mapped distant lands.

## Tudor firsts

The Tudors lived over 400 years ago, but we still use some of their inventions and do many of the same things they did. For example, did you know that the **flushing toilet** and the pencil were invented in Tudor times? Or that the Tudors were the first people in Britain to eat potatoes, play tennis, and visit shopping centres?

During Tudor times the city of London grew very fast. Some Tudor buildings still survive in London today. A copy of Shakespeare's Globe Theatre has been built in modern London, in the same spot as the Tudor theatre.

# Tudor kings and queens

Henry VII was the first Tudor **monarch**. He was crowned in 1485 after he won the **Wars of the Roses**. He died in 1509, and his son Henry VIII became king.

Henry VIII had six wives and three children, called Mary, Elizabeth, and Edward. When Henry died in 1547, Edward was crowned king. He was only nine years old, but because he was a boy he was first in line to the throne. After he died in 1553, aged only 15, his older sister Mary became Queen.

This portrait of Elizabeth I was painted in 1559. It shows her in the special clothes that she wore when she was crowned queen.

## THEN...

Elizabeth I was only 25 years old when she became queen. She ruled for the next 45 years. At the time, most people thought that women were too weak to rule a country. Elizabeth proved them wrong. During her long reign, she made England strong and united, and helped many writers, merchants, and explorers. Elizabeth I became a model for future monarchs.

Mary ruled for five years. She wanted to make a lot of changes in England, but died in 1558, before she had the chance to make much difference. Mary's younger sister Elizabeth then became queen. Many people have called Elizabeth's reign a "golden age" in English history.

Elizabeth had no children to **inherit** the throne after her. When she died in 1603, the reign of the Tudor family came to an end.

Here, Queen Elizabeth II can be seen greeting crowds as she celebrates being on the throne for 50 years.

## ...NOW

Like the first Elizabeth, Queen Elizabeth II became queen when she was very young. She was crowned at the age of 26. Elizabeth II has been a popular monarch and has helped to unite her people. Everywhere she goes, she attracts huge crowds of cheering people, just like Elizabeth I.

# What was daily life like in Tudor times?

Rich people in Tudor times lived in large, comfortable houses. Life was very different for the poor. In the countryside, poor people lived in huts or tiny cottages. In towns, whole families were often squeezed together in a single room.

Padded chairs and detailed tapestries such as these were often found in the homes of rich Tudor families.

## THEN...

In Tudor times, furniture began to change. Instead of sitting on hard wooden chairs, as people had done in the Middle Ages, they sat on cushions, or padded the seats, arms, and backs of their chairs with cloth. Padded seats for two or more people were known as settles, and were very popular. The Tudor padded settles can be seen as a very early form of sofa.

This is a grand Tudor house built from beams and plaster. This striking method of house-building has been copied in some modern mock-Tudor homes.

## Tudor homes

The homes of kings and nobles were usually built from brick or stone. Most people's houses were made from a frame of wooden beams filled in with plaster. The rich could afford windows that opened using a latch. The windows were filled with small panes of glass. Poorer people could not afford glass.

The style of house-building invented by the Tudors is still popular today. People often build modern homes with oak beams and plaster. These houses are called "mock-Tudor".

## ...NOW

Today, most modern homes have very comfortable padded armchairs and sofas. In Tudor times, chairs were stuffed with horsehair, while today's furniture is usually padded with foam. Thanks to the Tudors, we no longer have to sit on hard wooden chairs, but they would still have been astonished at how comfortable our furniture has become!

# Baths and toilets

Very few Tudor houses had bathrooms or indoor toilets. Most people washed in tubs of water, but Henry VIII had a special bath built for him at Hampton Court Palace.

## Tudor deodorant

Even rich people in Tudor times did not wash very often. Instead, many ladies carried an orange with spicy-smelling cloves stuck into it. They hoped that the strong smell of the cloves would hide their body odour and protect them against illnesses!

This is a Tudor close stool. It was like a chair with a **chamber pot** in the seat.

## THEN...

Around 1590, Sir John Harington invented the **flushing toilet**. This was a "water closet" with levers that sent water from a tank into the toilet to flush it out. Queen Elizabeth was impressed by Harington's invention, but it was another 250 years before most people began to use water closets.

This portrait was painted in 1593 and shows the type of clothes worn by Tudor noblemen. The man is wearing a ruff around his neck and a silk ribbon on his arm for decoration.

## Clothes and make-up

Poor people in Tudor times wore simple clothes made from rough wool. Royalty and nobles dressed in fine clothes made from silk, velvet, and cotton. The silk came from India, and cotton came from India and Egypt.

Some Tudor women wore very heavy make-up. When she grew old, Queen Elizabeth I covered her face with a thick white paste and painted her cheeks and lips bright red. The paste was made from lead, which was later found to be poisonous.

### ...NOW

Modern toilets work in a similar way to Harrington's water closet. Today, most toilets are linked to **sewage pipes** that carry the waste away, but the Tudors had no sewage system. People in towns often threw the contents of their chamber pots into the street, where they spread diseases.

# How were the Tudors educated?

The Tudor period was an important time for learning. The Tudor monarchs built many schools and university colleges. William Caxton had set up the first printing press in England in 1476. He printed most of the books he published in English rather than Latin or French. This meant that more books could be read by more people.

This Bible was printed in 1539. It was less expensive to print books than to copy them out by hand. This allowed many more people to read them.

## THEN...

Grammar schools were a Tudor invention. Before the Tudor period, only a few boys could be taught by priests or tutors. The Tudor grammar schools provided the chance for large numbers of pupils to have a good education. Pupils learned Latin grammar, public speaking, and arithmetic.

## Tudor education

Boys and girls from wealthy families were taught at home by a tutor, but only boys could go to school. When they were about five years old, some boys were sent to the village "petty school" where they learned to read and write. At the age of seven, boys from well-off families went on to a "grammar school". Boys from poor families left school and learned a trade.

The cleverest grammar school boys went on to university at Oxford or Cambridge. In Tudor times, boys could start university at 14 years of age!

This is the school room of the grammar school where the playwright William Shakespeare was taught in the 1570s.

## ...NOW

Today, everyone in Britain – boys and girls, rich and poor – can go to school. There are many different kinds of school, and many more subjects to study. Only a few schools still teach Latin.

# What did the Tudors do for entertainment?

Tudor England was a good place for poets, musicians, and artists. They gathered at the court and received royal help and support.

## William Shakespeare

The greatest writer of the Elizabethan age was William Shakespeare. He wrote 37 plays and over 150 poems. Today, Shakespeare's plays are performed all over the world. We use many of his lines every day. The sayings: "heart of gold", "too much of a good thing", and "a wild goose chase" all come from Shakespeare's work.

This is an illustration of what Shakespeare's Globe theatre may have looked like. There was no roof over the stage and the "pit", so everyone got wet when it rained!

## THEN...

Seeing plays was a popular form of entertainment in Tudor times. The theatres were round and made from wood. They had a raised stage, with seats around three sides. In front of the stage was the "pit", where poorer people could stand. Snacks were sold in stalls outside, and people ate pies while they watched the play.

These modern actors are performing William Shakespeare's play *The Tempest* in an outdoor theatre.

## Smelly audiences

Elizabethan theatres could get very hot. The members of the audience who stood to watch plays were known as the "groundlings". In summer, they were also known as the "stinkards"!

## ...NOW

People in Britain still love going to the theatre. Many modern theatres follow the Tudor model, with seats on three sides of the stage. People still buy treats, such as ice-cream, to eat during the interval. However, unlike the Tudors, they no longer throw their food at the stage when they don't like the acting!

15

## Having fun

The Tudors knew how to enjoy themselves! Kings and nobles went hunting and took part in the sport of **falconry**. They held feasts, with musicians and clowns called jesters to entertain them.

People of all ages played games such as cards and chess. Tudor children played with dolls and balls, and rolled wooden hoops along the ground.

These Tudor tennis players are shown playing in a court much like Henry VIII's court at Hampton Court Palace.

## THEN...

Tennis was first played in England in Tudor times. It was King Henry VIII's favourite game and he had a court built for him at Hampton Court Palace. Tudor tennis was played in a court with high walls, like a modern squash court. Players used a wooden racket and a leather ball, which was stuffed with human hair.

Some Tudor entertainments were cruel and violent. Crowds went to fairs to see dancing bears, fighting cocks, and wrestling matches. **Jousting tournaments**, in which knights showed off their skills, had begun in the Middle Ages, and were still popular.

Next time you play cards, take a good look at the king, queen, jack, and joker. They are all based on figures in the Tudor court.

## ...NOW

Since Tudor times, tennis has gone through many changes. The Tudors played in their everyday clothes, but modern tennis players wear loose clothing and special shoes. Henry VIII would have been stunned at the speed of the modern game, played with lightweight rackets and rubber-filled balls.

## Painting portraits

During the Tudor period, artists began to paint life-like **portraits**. When King Henry VIII planned to marry Anne of Cleves, a German princess he had never met, he asked the painter Hans Holbein to travel to Germany to paint a portrait of her. He had no other way of finding out what she looked like.

Hans Holbein's painting of Anne of Cleves may have made her look prettier than she really was. When King Henry met her, he thought she was ugly, but he still married her.

THEN...

In the 1560s, shepherds in Cumbria, in northern England, discovered a coal-like rock that was useful for marking sheep. It was graphite, but at first people thought it was lead. Soon, Tudor artists started using "lead pencils". They wrapped a stick of graphite in string or sheepskin and used it to draw with.

## Tudor music

Music was played and enjoyed by people of all classes. Boys and girls from rich families learned to play the lute (an instrument similar to the guitar), the recorder, or the virginals (an early type of keyboard instrument). Poorer people often played bagpipes or flutes.

Wealthy people sang madrigals. These were songs that had parts for three to six different voices. Poorer people sang folk songs, which were handed down from parent to child. Some Tudor songs, such as *Greensleeves*, are still sung today.

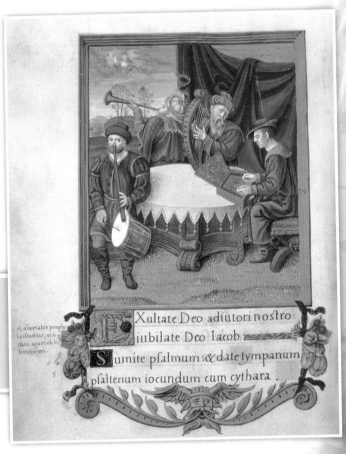

This illustration of Tudor musicians is from a book made during the reign of Henry VIII.

## ...NOW

By the 1700s, people had started to use a wooden case to hold the "lead" in pencils. Erasers were added to the tops of some pencils in the 1850s. Propelling pencils, which hold a thin stick of graphite that can be moved up and down, were invented in 1822. Some of the world's best pencils are still made in Cumbria.

# How did society change under the Tudors?

English society went through many changes in the Tudor period. Towns grew and **merchants** became very rich. Nobles and bishops lost a lot of their power, and the English Church changed forever.

King Henry VIII is famous for marrying six times. Henry's plan to divorce his first wife led to his quarrel with the Roman Catholic Church.

## THEN...

After Henry VIII's quarrel with the Pope, Roman Catholic churches were taken over by the Church of England. Henry made no changes to the church buildings, but he raided the country's **monasteries** and left them in ruins. He claimed that the monks were leading sinful lives, but he also wanted their land and riches.

# Changes in the Church

After 17 years of marriage to Catherine of Aragon, Henry still did not have a son to be king after him. He made plans to divorce Catherine and marry Anne Boleyn. This led to a bitter quarrel with the Pope, the head of the Roman Catholic Church. The Pope refused to allow Henry to divorce Catherine.

In 1534, Henry broke away from the Catholics and made himself head of a new Church, the Church of England. He no longer had to get permission to divorce Catherine. Many people were furious with Henry, but there was little they could do.

Fountains Abbey in Yorkshire was a very important monastery until King Henry VIII gave orders to raid it.

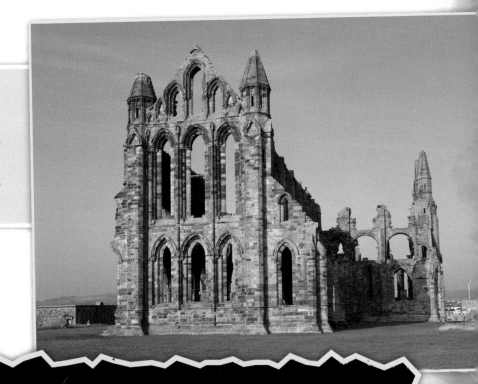

...NOW

The Church of England still has the British **monarch** as its head. It is often known as the Anglican Church, and has followers in many parts of the world. Some ruined monasteries can still be found in the British countryside. They remind us of the time that Henry stripped the monks of their wealth.

## Changes in the countryside

During the Tudor period, the **medieval** way of farming broke down. People no longer worked on enormous fields that belonged to their local lord. Instead, they began to farm small patches of land of their own. In place of the large, open fields of medieval times, the land became a patchwork of tiny fields, surrounded by hedges and walls.

## Tudor towns

Towns grew fast in Tudor times. For example, the population of London rose from around 50,000 in 1500 to over 200,000 in 1600. Towns became crowded and noisy. The streets were lined with shops and stalls, and were filled with people hurrying about their business.

### Near neighbours

Some streets in Tudor London were so narrow that people could lean out of their windows and shake hands with the person living opposite!

## THEN...

During the reign of Elizabeth I, the first shopping centre was built in London, above the area where the bankers and **merchants** met. There were more than 100 shops under one roof, and lots of stalls selling pies and other snacks. People had to watch out for **pickpockets** in the crowd.

We can thank the Tudors for the clever idea of putting lots of small shops together under one roof.

## ...NOW

Shopping centres are found all over the world and can be enormous. They have hundreds of shops and restaurants. They are light and clean, unlike the Tudor streets, and have security cameras everywhere to help catch thieves.

# Where did the Tudors explore and trade?

The Tudors were famous for their sailing skills. Henry VIII and Elizabeth I built up the navy and made it strong. In 1588, when Elizabeth I was queen, England was saved from attack when its navy defeated the **Spanish Armada**. The armada was a large group of ships sent by the king of Spain to attack England. After the Tudor period, the British navy continued to grow and become respected around the world.

## Tudor explorers

Many sailors travelled west from England, looking for a new route to India that would mean ships did not have to sail all the way around Africa. In 1497, John Cabot reached Newfoundland, in Canada. In the 1570s, Martin Frobisher explored the east coast of Canada, and in 1580, Sir Francis Drake became the first Englishman to sail around the world. These Tudor captains were the first in a long line of British explorers.

## THEN...

In the Tudor period, maps became more accurate than they had been before. Around 1512, Henry VIII employed Sebastian Cabot, the son of John Cabot, as his mapmaker. In 1569, a Flemish (Belgian) mapmaker called Gerardus Mercator printed a world map. A year later, the first world atlas was published. The atlas was a book that had maps of all the world's countries that were known at that time.

This painting shows one of Henry VIII's largest ships, the *Mary Rose*. The *Mary Rose* sank in 1545 but was raised to the surface in 1982 and is now in a museum.

## ...NOW

For 400 years after the Tudor period, people made maps in the same way. Explorers made careful measurements, then copied them on to charts. In the 20th century, however, satellite cameras changed everything. Modern mapmakers can use photographs taken from space to make very accurate maps of the world.

## Links with America

One of the most important things the Tudors did was to create links between England and North America. Starting with John Cabot in 1497, many Tudor explorers travelled along the American coast. In the 1580s, Sir Walter Raleigh tried to create **colonies** of English settlers on Roanoke Island, off the coast of North Carolina.

Raleigh's colonies failed, but in 1607 an English colony was set up at Jamestown in Virginia. This was the first of a group of states that would later become the United States of America.

Sir Walter Raleigh took his first group of settlers to North America in 1584. This painting shows an artist's idea of what happened when he landed.

## THEN...

Tudor explorers and **merchants** brought back many foods from North and South America. No one in England had ever seen such things as potatoes, tomatoes, sweetcorn, chillies, and pineapples before. Potatoes and tomatoes could be grown in England and soon became an important part of the English diet. Pineapples were a luxury, and were only eaten by the very rich.

## Smoking leaves

In the 1560s, English captains brought back tobacco plants from America. When people realized that they could smoke the leaves, the fashion for smoking took off!

These are some examples of the types of fruit and vegetables that were brought to Britain from America during Tudor times.

## ...NOW

In modern Britain, people eat all kinds of American foods. Tudor ships took months to carry food and plants back to England, but now fruit and vegetables are flown across the Atlantic in a few hours. Cacao beans, which are used for making chocolate, come from South America. They first arrived in England in Tudor times, but the Tudors only used them in medicines!

# Key dates

Here is an outline of important moments in the history and culture of Tudor England:

| | |
|---|---|
| 1485 | Henry Tudor is crowned King Henry VII |
| 1497 | John Cabot reaches Newfoundland and explores the coast |
| 1509 | Henry VII dies and his 17-year-old son is crowned King Henry VIII |
| around 1512 | Sebastian Cabot works as Henry VIII's mapmaker |
| 1534 | Henry VIII declares himself head of the Church in England |
| 1536 | Henry VIII starts stripping the **monasteries** of their wealth |
| 1547 | Henry VIII dies and his nine-year-old son is crowned King Edward VI |
| 1553 | Edward VI dies, aged 15. After the nine-day reign of Lady Jane Grey, Edward's sister Mary is crowned. |
| 1558 | Mary I dies, aged 42. Her sister Elizabeth is crowned. |

| | |
|---|---|
| around 1560 | English shepherds discover graphite, which is used to make pencils |
| 1569 | Gerardus Mercator prints his map of the world |
| 1576 | Martin Frobisher makes his first voyage to the east coast of Canada |
| 1580 | Sir Francis Drake returns from sailing around the world |
| 1584 | Sir Walter Raleigh attempts to create an English **colony** in North America |
| 1588 | The English navy defeats the **Spanish Armada** |
| around 1590 | Sir John Harington invents the **flushing toilet** |
| around 1590 | William Shakespeare writes his first play |
| 1599 | The Globe Theatre in London is opened |
| 1603 | Elizabeth I dies, aged 69. James I becomes king. |

# Glossary

**bladder** organ in the body in which urine (wee) is stored before it leaves the body. Pigs' bladders were used to make the first footballs.

**chamber pot** shallow china pot with a handle that is used as a toilet. In the past, people often kept a chamber pot under their bed at night.

**colony** land that has been settled by people from a different country

**falconry** hunting sport, in which trained birds of prey, called falcons, hunt and kill smaller birds, then bring them back to their owners

**flushing toilet** toilet with a handle that makes water flow quickly through the toilet bowl and wash the waste away

**inherit** take over something from another person after they have died

**jousting tournaments** mock battles, in which two knights on horseback charge at each other, and each tries to knock the other off his horse

**medieval** to do with the Middle Ages, a period in history that lasted from around AD 500 to around 1485

**merchant** someone who buys and sells goods

**monarch** king or queen

**monastery** place where monks live and practise their religion

**pickpocket** someone who steals by reaching into people's pockets or bags in crowded places

**portrait** painting or drawing of someone, usually of their face or upper body

**sewage pipes** pipes that carry waste underground to a special plant, where the waste is treated to make it clean and safe

**Spanish Armada** large group of ships sent by the king of Spain to attack England in 1588

**Wars of the Roses** series of battles from 1455 to 1487, fought between two powerful English noble families, the Yorks and the Lancasters, to gain control of the English throne

# Find out more

## Books

*Discover the Tudors: Tudor Exploration*, Moira Butterfield (Franklin Watts, 2010)

*Discover the Tudors: Tudor Theatre*, Moira Butterfield (Franklin Watts, 2010)

*History from Objects: The Tudors*, Angela Royston (Wayland, 2010)

*Unlocking History: Life in Tudor Times*, Brian Williams (Heinemann Library, 2009)

## Websites

**www.historyonthenet.com/Tudors/tudorsmain.htm**
This website has lots of information on the Tudor period, including kings and queens, food, clothes, and entertainment.

**www.tudorbritain.org**
This is a fun website about Tudor life, including lots of activities for you to try.

**www.tudorhistory.org**
On this website, you can find recordings of Tudor music and actors reading from Tudor books. There are also pictures and information about Tudor life.

## Places to visit

Hampton Court Palace
www.hrp.org.uk/HamptonCourtPalace

Mary Rose Museum
www.maryrose.org

Tower of London
www.hrp.org.uk/TowerOfLondon

# Index

Anglican Church 21
Anne of Cleves 18
atlases 24

bagpipes 19
baths 10
Boleyn, Anne 21

Cabot, John 24, 26
Cabot, Sebastian 24
cacao beans 27
cards 17
Catherine of
   Aragon 21
Caxton, William 12
chamber pots 11
Church of England
   20, 21
clothes 10, 17
colonies 26

daily life 8–11
deodorants 11
divorce 21
Drake, Sir Francis 24

education 12–13
Edward VI 6
Elizabeth I 6, 7,
   10, 24
Elizabeth II 7
entertainment 14–17
exploration 24, 26

fairs 17
falconry 16
farming 22
feasts 16

flutes 19
folk songs 19
food 26, 27
football 17
Fountains Abbey 21
Frobisher, Martin 24
furniture 8, 9

games 16
Globe Theatre 4, 14
grammar schools
   12, 13
graphite 18
groundlings 15

Hampton Court
   Palace 10, 14
Harington, Sir John
   10, 11
Henry VII 6
Henry VIII 6, 10, 16,
   17, 18, 20, 21, 24
Holbein, Hans 18
homes 8–9

jousting 17

Latin 12, 13
lead pencils 18, 19
Little Moreton Hall 8
London 22

make-up 10
maps 24, 25
Mary 6, 7
merchants 20, 22
monasteries 20, 21
music 19

navy 24
North America 24, 26

portraits 18
printing press 12
propelling pencils 19

Raleigh, Sir Walter 26
Roman Catholic
   Church 20, 21

satellite cameras 25
schools 12, 13
settles 8
sewage systems 11
Shakespeare,
   William 4, 13, 14
shopping centres
   22, 23
social change 20–23
sofas 8, 9
Spanish Armada 24

tennis 16, 17
theatres 14–15
thieves 22, 23
toilets 10, 11
towns 22
Tudor kings and
   queens 6–7

universities 12, 13

virginals 19

Wars of the Roses 6
women 6, 10